I Found a Friend in You

PAINTINGS BY

Judy Buswell

HARVEST HOUSE PUBLISHERS

EUGENE, OREGON

I Found a Friend in You

Text Copyright © 2005 by Harvest House Publishers
Eugene, Oregon 97402

ISBN-13: 978-0-7369-1551-9
ISBN-10: 0-7369-1551-6

Design and production by Garborg Design Works, Minneapolis, Minnesota

Scripture quotations are taken from the King James Version of the Bible.

Harvest House Publishers has made every effort to trace the ownership of all poems and quotes. In the event of a question arising from the use of a poem or quote, we regret any error made and will be pleased to make the necessary correction in future editions of this book.

Printed in China

11 12 13 14 15 / LP / 11 10 9 8 7

To:

Holly Keast

Merry Christmas!

With Love,

Holly Maloy

How wonderful to have found a friend in you!

The best relationships…are built up like a fine lacquer finish, with accumulated layers made of many little acts of love. And like a lacquer finish, love grows more and more beautiful with each additional layer.

DAVE GILBERT

Friends are flowers
that never fade away.

AUTHOR UNKNOWN

That peculiar motion
of the heart, that
secret joining of hands,
is based upon something
deep and vital,
some spiritual kinship,
some subtle likeness.

ARTHUR C. BENSON

Joy is an essential ingredient of
intimacy. Without joy—not the
manufactured sensation or frantic
scurrying, but the contentment that
surprises—there is not time or place
for the amazed lingering that is the
heart and mystery of intimacy.

JANE OLTHIUS

*B*ut I gathered that there was a region in which the heart could be entirely absorbed in a deep and beautiful admiration for some other soul, and rejoice whole-heartedly in its nobleness and greatness; so that no question of gaining anything, or even of being helped to anything, came in, any more than one who has long been pent in shadow and gloom and illness, and comes out for the first time into the sun, thinks of the benefits that he may receive from the caressing sunlight; he merely knows that it is joy and happiness and life to be there, and to feel the warm light comfort him and make him glad.

ARTHUR C. BENSON

*B*ut remember this, when we make the biggest fools of ourselves that is precisely the time when we need friends, and when they stick to us the tightest, if they are worthwhile.

GENE STRATTON-PORTER

A best friend is a
sister that destiny
forgot to give you.

AUTHOR UNKNOWN

A friendship can weather most things
and thrive in thin soil—but it needs a
little mulch of letters and phone calls
and small silly presents every so often—
just to save it from drying out.

PAM BROWN

I am glad that in the springtime of life there were those who

To have you know my weaknesses is a hard thing. To have you know my weaknesses and still love me is a great thing.

JEANNE SHERIDAN

People are like islands. Sometimes you have to row around them to know where to land.

LLOYD J. OGILVIE

planted flowers of love in my heart instead of thistles.

ROBERT LOUIS STEVENSON

Breathless, we flung us on the windy hill,
Laughed in the sun, and kissed the lovely grass.

RUPERT BROOKE

Good friends are good for your health.

IRWIN SARASON

The better part of one's life consists of his friendships.

ABRAHAM LINCOLN

You are as welcome
as flowers in May.

CHARLES MACKLIN

11

*T*he only thing that makes
one place more attractive to
me than another is the
quantity of heart I find in it.

JANE WELSH CARLYLE

*Kindred spirits go together
like white on rice.*

CATHERINE TILNEY

*T*rue friends visit us in
prosperity only when invited,
but in adversity they come
without invitation.

THEOPHRASTUS

Life is to be fortified by many friendships.
To love and to be loved is the greatest
happiness of existence.

SYDNEY SMITH

One's duty is to encourage and believe in one's friend, not to disapprove of and to censure him. One loves him for what he is, not for what he might be if he would only take one's advice. The point is that it must be all a free gift, not a mutual improvement society. The secure friendship is that which begins in comradeship, and moves into a more generous and emotional region. Then there is no need to demand or to question loyalty, because the tie has been welded by many a simple deed, many a frank word. The ideal is a perfect frankness and sincerity, which lays bare the soul as it is, without any false shame or any fear of misunderstanding. A friendship of this kind can be one of the purest, brightest, and strongest things in the world. Yet how rare it is!

ARTHUR C. BENSON
"FRIENDSHIP"
PUTNAM'S MONTHLY, 1907

True friends make every landing softer.

JEANNE SHERIDAN

15

A friend is known
when needed. ARABIAN PROVERB

*I*t is a great thing to have friends
when one is young, but indeed
it is still more so when you are
getting old. When we are young,
friends are, like everything else,
a matter of course. In the old
days, we know what it means
to have them.

EDVARD GRIEG

I have always been delighted at
the prospect of a new day, a fresh
try, one more start, with perhaps
a bit of magic waiting somewhere
behind the morning.

J.B. PRIESTLY

17

*We need old friends to help us grow old
and new friends to help us stay young.*

LETTY COTTIN POGREBIN

I confess that, for myself, I never enter a new company without the hope that I may discover a friend, perhaps *the* friend, sitting there with an expectant smile.

ARTHUR C. BENSON

*W*e take care of our health, we lay up money, we make our roof tight and our clothing sufficient, but who provides wisely that he shall not be wanting the best property of all—friends?

RALPH WALDO EMERSON

*Friends and good manners will
carry you where money won't go.*

MARGARET WALKER

I am speaking now of the highest duty we owe our friends, the noblest, the most sacred—that of keeping their own nobleness, goodness, pure and incorrupt.

HARRIET BEECHER STOWE

The man who treasures his friends is usually solid gold himself.

MARJORIE HOLMES

*T*he only good teachers for you are those friends who love you, who think you are interesting, or very important, or wonderfully funny.

BRENDA UELAND

*T*reat your friends as you do your pictures, and place them in their best light.

JENNIE JEROME CHURCHILL

It is wise to apply the oil of refined politeness to the mechanism of friendship.

COLETTE

*F*riends are the thermometer by which we may judge the temperature of our fortunes.

LADY MARGUERITE BLESSINGTON

Best friend, my
well-spring in
the wilderness!

GEORGE ELIOT

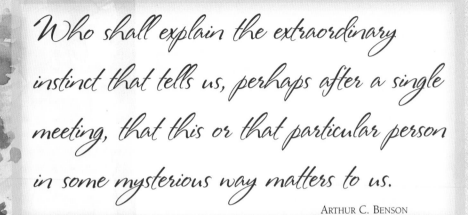

Who shall explain the extraordinary instinct that tells us, perhaps after a single meeting, that this or that particular person in some mysterious way matters to us.

ARTHUR C. BENSON

My only sketch, profile, of Heaven is a large blue sky, and larger than the biggest I have seen in June—and in it are my friends—every one of them.

EMILY DICKINSON

A home-made friend wears longer than one you buy in the market.

AUSTIN O'MALLEY

25

You don't just luck into things as much as you'd like to think you do. You build step by step, whether it's friendship or opportunities.

BARBARA BUSH

Could we see when and where we would meet again, we would be more tender when we bid our friends goodbye.

OUIDA

*I*t's what each one of us sows, and how, that gives to us character and prestige. Seeds of kindness, goodwill, and human understanding, planted in fertile soil, spring up into deathless friendships, big deeds of worth, and a memory that will not soon fade…

GEORGE MATTHEW ADAMS

*Friendship without self-interest
is one of the rare and
beautiful things of life.*

JAMES F. BYRNES

If I were to name the
three most precious
resources of life, I
should say books,
friends, and nature…

JOHN BURROUGHS

Some of the richest
friendships of all are
friendships between
people whose whole
view of life is sharply
contrasted.

ARTHUR C. BENSON

*Greater love hath no man than this, that
a man lay down his life for his friends.*

THE BOOK OF JOHN

$\mathcal{N}$o love, no
friendship can
cross the path
of our destiny
without leaving
some mark on
it forever.

FRANÇOIS MAURIAC

$\mathcal{W}$ishing to be
friends is quick
work, but friendship
is a slow-ripening
fruit.

ARISTOTLE

Nobody sees a flower really; it is so small. We haven't time, and to see takes time—like to have a friend takes time.

GEORGIA O'KEEFFE

31

A single rose can be
my garden...a single
friend, my world.

Leo Buscaglia

Friendship is

the only thing

in the world

concerning the

usefulness of

which all

mankind are

agreed.

MARCUS CICERO

Friends are as companions on a journey, who ought to aid each other to persevere in the road to a happier life.

PYTHAGORAS

Our friends interpret the world and ourselves to us, if we take them tenderly and truly.

AMOS BRONSON ALCOTT

33

Perhaps the most delightful friendships are those in which there is much agreement, much disputation, and yet more personal liking.

GEORGE ELIOT

"Miss Barry was a kindred spirit, after all," Anne confided to Marilla. "You wouldn't think so to look at her, but she is. You don't find it right out at first, as in Matthew's case, but after a while you come to see it. Kindred spirits are not so scarce as I used to think. It's splendid to find out there are so many of them in the world."

L. M. MONTGOMERY
ANNE OF GREEN GABLES

Strange how
brave it makes
you to belong.

ELEANOR KELLY

It would be a lonesome thing to see our own little orb spinning around through space alone, with no sun, nor moon, nor stars to keep it in countenance. There they are, out there, the great company of the heavenly host, working together in harmony, bound by an invisible, insoluble band, so frail, so tenuous we are hardly aware of it, and yet never loosened.

AUTHOR UNKNOWN

Friendship is a compact in which one fairly shares defects and merits.

GUY DE MAUPASSANT

*B*ut the fact remains that there are unnumbered relationships between all sorts of apparently incongruous persons, of which the basis is not physical desire, or the protective instinct, and is not built up upon any hope of gain or profit whatsoever. All sorts of qualities may lend a hand to strengthen and increase and confirm these bonds; but what lies at the base of all is simply a sort of vital congeniality. The friend is the person whom one is in need of, and by whom one is needed. Life is a sweeter, stronger, fuller, more gracious thing for the friend's existence, whether he be near or far; if the friend is close at hand, that is best; but if he is far away he is still there, to think of, to wonder about, to hear from, to write to, to share life and experience with, to serve, to honor, to admire, to love.

ARTHUR C. BENSON
"FRIENDSHIP"
PUTNAM'S MONTHLY, 1907

Everyone
appreciates
a friend.

HELEN ROBERTS

The soul of Jonathan was knit to the soul of David and Jonathan loved him as his own soul.

THE BOOK OF 1 SAMUEL

An adequate companionship is the rarest gift of life; to lose it is to bear the greatest human sorrow and thereby to be open to the greatest exaltation.

AUTHOR UNKNOWN

41

In friendships, there must be no reserve; as much deliberation as you please before the league is struck, but no doubtings nor jealousies after...It requires time to consider a friendship, but the resolution once taken entitles him to my very heart...The purpose of friendship is to have one dearer to me than myself, and for the saving of whose life I would gladly lay down my own, taking with the consciousness that only the wise can be friends; others are mere companions.

SENECA

You must not mind my speaking quite plainly to you. Of course I should not dream of doing so if I were not your friend. But what is the good of friendship if one cannot say exactly what one means?

OSCAR WILDE

Ain't it good when life seems dreary
And your hopes about to end,
Just to feel the handclasp cheery
Of a fine old loyal friend?

EDGAR A. GUEST

*H*erbert received me with open arms, and I had never felt before, so blessedly, what it is to have a friend.

CHARLES DICKENS
GREAT EXPECTATIONS

Finally, be ye all of one mind, having compassion one of another, love as brethren, be pitiful, be courteous.

THE BOOK OF 1 PETER

*F*rom fearing Mrs. Ruffner I soon learned to look upon her as one of my best friends…Mrs. Ruffner always encouraged and sympathized with me in all my efforts to get an education.

BOOKER T. WASHINGTON
UP FROM SLAVERY

45

When you find a friend in trouble
Pass along a word of cheer.
Often it is very helpful
Just to feel a friend is near.

THORNTON W. BURGESS
MRS. PETER RABBIT

There must be genuine love of the neighbor, before there can be a love of God; for neighborly love is the ground in which that higher and purer love takes root.

T.S. ARTHUR

"Suppose we try kindness," suggested the Tin Woodman. "I've heard that anyone can be conquered with kindness, no matter how ugly they may be."

L. FRANK BAUM
*THE MARVELOUS
LAND OF OZ*

What is the will of God?—to do to my fellow man what I would have my fellow man to do to me—that is the will of God.

HERMAN MELVILLE
MOBY DICK

46

On meeting his old friend, Joseph Mouradour, at a ball, M. de Meroul was filled with a deep and simple joy, for in their youth they had been intimate friends.

GUY DE MAUPASSANT
"FRIEND JOSEPH"